140
miles

For Katie, Tamara, and John —D. S.

This one is for August Gardiner Friedberg,
the newest member of the family —J. H.

SIMON & SCHUSTER BOOKS FOR YOUNG READERS
An imprint of Simon & Schuster Children's Publishing Division • 1230 Avenue of the Americas, New York, New York 10020

The text for this book was set in Caslon Classico. • The illustrations for this book were rendered in gouache.
Manufactured in China • 0525 SCP • First Edition
2 4 6 8 10 9 7 5 3 1
CIP data for this book is available from the Library of Congress.
ISBN 9781665926409 • ISBN 9781665926416 (ebook)

The High-Flying, Deep-Diving Adventures of Kathy Sullivan

Astronaut and Oceanographer

Written by Diane Stanley

Illustrated by Jessie Hartland

A Paula Wiseman Book
Simon & Schuster Books for Young Readers
New York • Amsterdam/Antwerp
London • Toronto
Sydney/Melbourne
New Delhi

It started with a map. Actually, a map PLUS the *National Geographic*s. They sort of worked together. The map showed Kathy all the places in the world: Cities and mountains. Deserts, islands, and jungles. Rivers, lakes, and oceans.

Then, once she knew where those places were, the magazines showed her what they looked like: exotic and beautiful and TOTALLY different from Paterson, New Jersey, where she lived. Someday she would visit those places and have grand adventures: climbing mountains, riding a camel through a desert—that sort of thing.

But there was one place Kathy never even *dreamed* of going—because it wasn't on her map.

N
3710
WORLD
MAP
ISLAND
T
M
G
key

But she would think of it soon—one dark October night in 1957, when she had just turned six. Her father called for Kathy and her brother to hurry outside. He had something exciting to show them.

They stood together on the lawn, and he pointed to the sky. "See that tiny light?" he said. And sure enough, there it was, moving slowly across the sky.

It wasn't a star, he told them. It was a *satellite*, made of shiny metal, no bigger than a beach ball. Soviet scientists had built it, named it Sputnik, and sent it into space. Now it was orbiting Earth like a tiny silver moon.

Space! Kathy thought. If Sputnik could go there, maybe people could too. And wouldn't that be **the most amazing adventure of all?**

Suddenly, America was in a Space Race with the Soviet Union—and the Soviets were ahead! So America started its own space agency, the National Aeronautics and Space Administration (which was a real mouthful, so everyone just called it NASA). It was busy building rocket ships, and it'd chosen seven astronauts to fly them. Kathy studied their pictures in *Life* magazine. They looked so heroic in their shiny silver space suits, posing for the camera like movie stars!

But she couldn't help noticing that all of them were men. Couldn't girls be astronauts too?

Fast-forward to July 20, 1969. Seventeen-year-old Kathy was sitting on the floor in front of the TV, waiting breathlessly for something to happen. Something that no human had ever done before, being broadcast live for all the world to see.

And then, at last, the great moment arrived. An American astronaut, Neil Armstrong, climbed slowly down the ladder of the lunar module. Paused. Then dropped softly onto the gray, dusty, pockmarked surface of the moon!

A man was actually standing on the moon!

And once again, that old yearning tugged at Kathy's heart—that longing for adventure, excitement, and discovery.

FESTIVAL
JAZZ
mission:
OUTER
SPACE!
CREAM
PILLOW

Then she took a college class in marine biology!

Her school was in California, near the ocean, so her class could go to the beach and study the shallow rock pools where water collected when the tide was high. These tide pools were teeming with exotic sea creatures. Starfish and sea urchins! Mussels and hermit crabs! And oh, the sea anemones—animals that looked like flowers or tiny trees, in beautiful, glowing colors!

What else, Kathy wondered, was out there beyond the shore or in the vast depths of the ocean? An enormous, amazing hidden world just waiting for her to discover it! At last Kathy had found her own great adventure:

she would be an oceanographer!

172
CSS HUDSON

Kathy studied oceans for nine years: first the Pacific during college, then the Atlantic for graduate school. Her favorite part was going out on research vessels to study the ocean floor, often spending months at sea. The ships were like floating science labs, with plenty of technology but not a lot of comfort. The trips could be rough, sometimes dangerous. But Kathy didn't care. She *loved* her work. It was everything she'd ever dreamed of.

But life is full of surprises. And, as Kathy would learn several times in her life, even the *best* of plans can change.

And that's exactly what happened one December when she went home for Christmas. There was her brother, waiting with exciting news: *NASA was starting a new space program!* It was for a different kind of spaceship, called a shuttle, that could carry people and satellites into orbit, then return to Earth and land on a runway like an ordinary plane. Soon NASA would be hiring astronauts to fly the shuttles. And—*wait for it!*—for the first time ever,

NASA was hiring women!

For a moment, Kathy could hardly breathe. Being an astronaut had never been a choice for her, just as space hadn't been on her map. Now, suddenly, it was! She knew her chances were probably one in ten thousand. But it couldn't hurt to apply.

One year later, early in the morning, the phone rang in the hallway of Kathy's apartment. It was one of the very top guys at NASA, and he was wondering if Kathy was still interested in being an astronaut.

Out of over eight thousand applicants, NASA had chosen thirty-five astronauts. Only six of them were women.

And Kathy was one of the six!

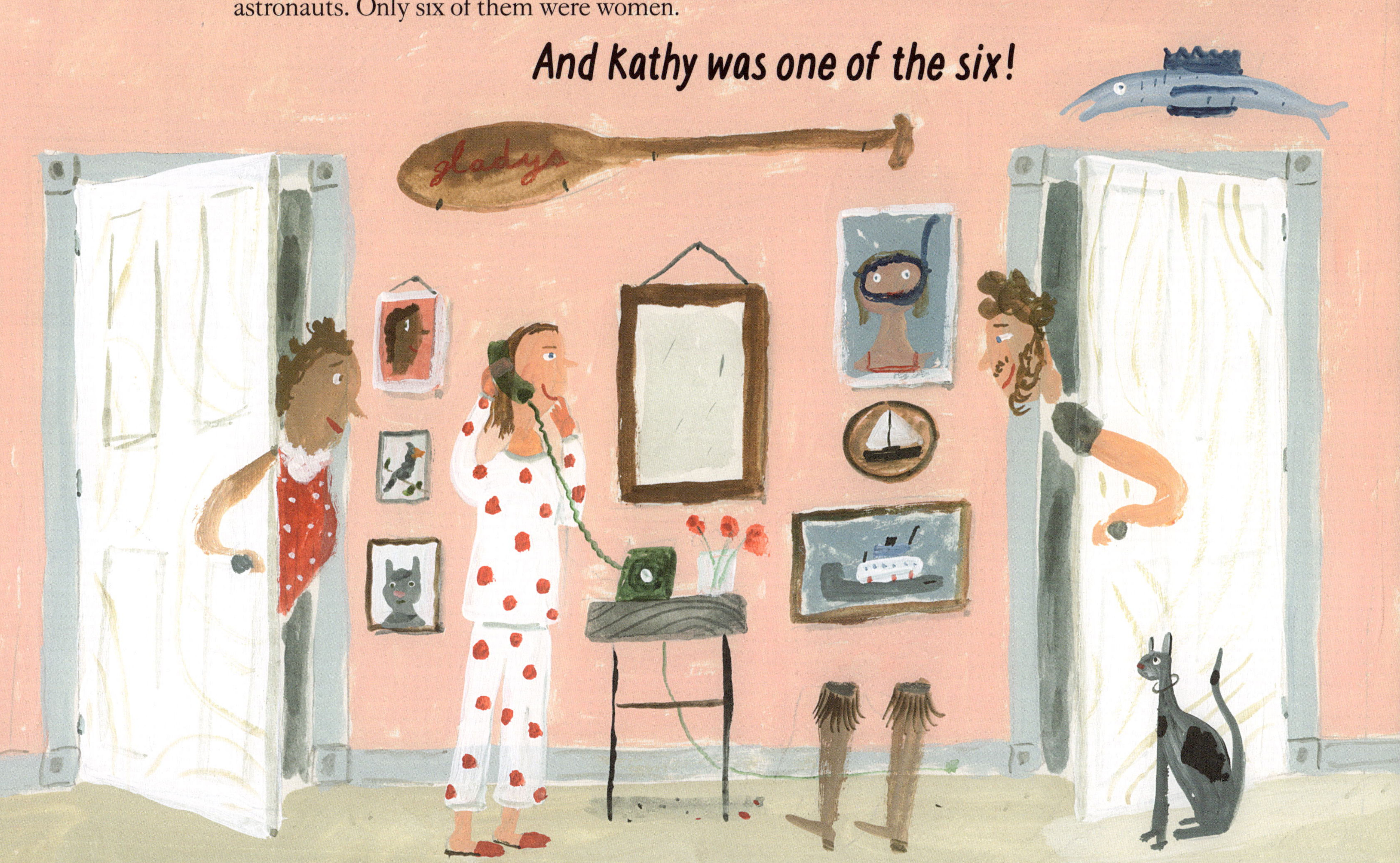

And so, after nine years of studying oceans and earning her PhD, Kathy moved to Houston to start all over again, training to be an astronaut.

And when her training was over, she got in line with everybody else, working at NASA and waiting for her chance to fly a mission. She would wait for another five years!

Then one summer, Kathy spent her vacation on a backpacking trip in Wyoming with friends. They hiked in the beautiful high country and slept out under the stars. But every few days, they'd check in with civilization at a friend's farm. That's where Kathy was when, once again, the phone rang and it was somebody from NASA.

She had finally been scheduled for a mission! But that wasn't all! She was about to become **the first American woman to walk in space!**

Kathy had to learn everything about the *Challenger* spacecraft, from the thousands of switches and dials on its console to how its electrical system worked. And to prepare for her spacewalk, she spent hours in NASA's giant neutral buoyancy pool.

The suit she wore, like the one she'd wear in space, weighed 225 pounds! It was so heavy, she had to be helped onto an elevator platform and lowered into the pool.

But once in the water, she floated, weightless, just as she would in space.

In the pool was a model of the fuel tank that she and her spacewalking partner, Dave Leestma, would be working on. Their mission was to prove that they could safely refuel a satellite in orbit. They practiced over and over, using the same special tools they'd have on the spacewalk and wearing the same big, clumsy gloves. When it came time to do it in space, it would all feel familiar and they'd be much more likely to do it right.

Finally the big day arrived. Kathy was dressed in her launch and entry suit—helmet on, visor down—and strapped into her seat. Then the final countdown started. It had taken her fifteen years to get to this moment. Now her great adventure was about to begin.

At ten seconds to liftoff, the voice of mission commander Robert Crippen came through her earphones:

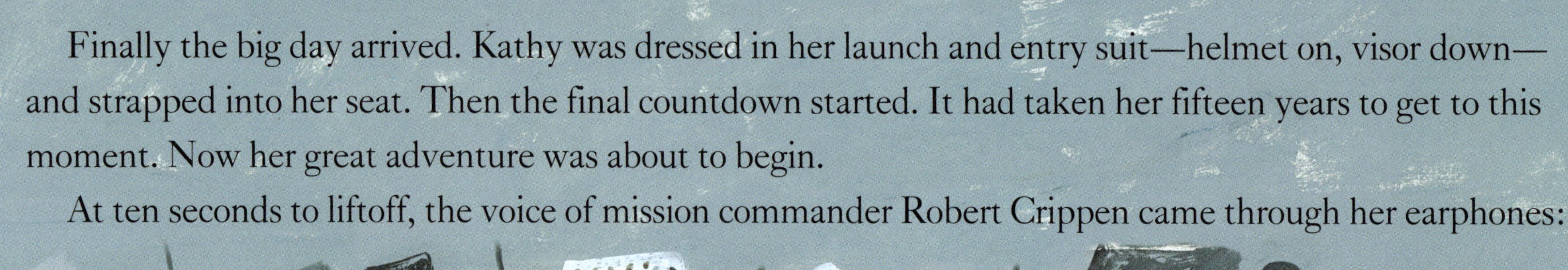

Then *Challenger* roared off the launchpad. Kathy was pressed hard against her seat as the shuttle rose, fighting its way through the atmosphere. The cockpit was a riot of noise: roaring, thumping, and rattling. It felt to Kathy like a "combination of earthquake, rock concert, and fighter jet." Or "eight and a half minutes of riding a bomb."

Then, suddenly, the cabin fell silent. The pressure vanished. Kathy's arms floated upward. Her checklist drifted off her lap. And for a moment nobody said a word. They didn't want to spoil the magic.

Living in space was like working in a really weird science lab, where no one went home at night and everything, including the scientists, tended to float around, so everything had to be strapped down. Even the meaning of day and night was different. The shuttle circled Earth every ninety minutes. Each time around brought a dark night and a bright day: *sixteen* of them in twenty-four hours!

But Kathy settled in quickly and went to work, helping to release a new satellite that would monitor Earth's atmosphere from space and doing a number of scientific tests. But there was one last experiment that had to be done *outside* the spacecraft. That would be Kathy's big moment.

Now she was waiting inside the air lock, dressed for space in her two-million-dollar pressurized suit. During her three-and-a-half-hour spacewalk, it would keep her alive, providing air to breathe, communication with Dave and the mission commander, and protection from the hazards of space—extreme heat and cold, radiation, and even meteoroids!

Then the air lock door opened, and Kathy swam out into the endless void of space. And suddenly there she was, clinging to a handrail on a spaceship traveling at 17,500 miles an hour, 140 miles above Earth, with only a tether connecting her to the shuttle.

Then the voice of Commander Crippen came through her earphones:

"Look around, guys," he said. "Appreciate where you are!"

NASA

Kathy flew three missions for NASA, spending more than 532 amazing hours in space. But two events would always stand out in her mind. The first, of course, was her spacewalk. The second was the mission on the space shuttle *Discovery* that carried the school bus–sized, twenty-four-thousand-pound, two-billion-dollar Hubble Telescope into space.

They took it as far beyond the distractions of Earth's atmosphere as the shuttle could safely go, a record-setting 380 miles above Earth. From there, the Hubble's camera could capture light from distant galaxies that had been traveling toward Earth for billions of years. It could *literally* look back in time! It would change what we know about the sun, the birth of stars, and the universe itself. Helping to launch the Hubble was the proudest moment of Kathy's career.

When her astronaut days were over, she used her knowledge in other ways, like running the National Oceanic and Atmospheric Administration (NOAA), the government agency you can thank for warning you about hurricanes.

But in saying yes to NASA all those years before, she'd given up another dream: to study the seafloor from a deep-ocean submersible. She'd made her choice and left that adventure behind, never dreaming she might get a second chance. But then—you guessed it—she got another call! This time it was from Victor Vescovo, an undersea explorer. Would Kathy like to be the first woman to visit the deepest part of the ocean?

Well, of course she would!

The Challenger Deep lies at the bottom of the Pacific Ocean's Mariana Trench, the lowest known point on Earth. At 35,872 feet below the ocean's surface, it's so deep that if you could pick up Mount Everest and drop it into the trench, its summit would still be more than a mile underwater!

Kathy would travel there in Victor's two-ton, full-ocean-depth submersible, a sort of miniaturized, space-age deep-ocean research vessel with a thick titanium pressure hull, four wide-angle cameras, equipment for collecting scientific samples and taking measurements—and two comfy leather seats for the pilot and his guest. It could travel to the bottom of the world and return in a single day.

The experience couldn't have been more different from blasting into space. It was like being inside a slowly descending magical sphere. No special suits were required, just comfortable clothes. They ate lunch on the way down.

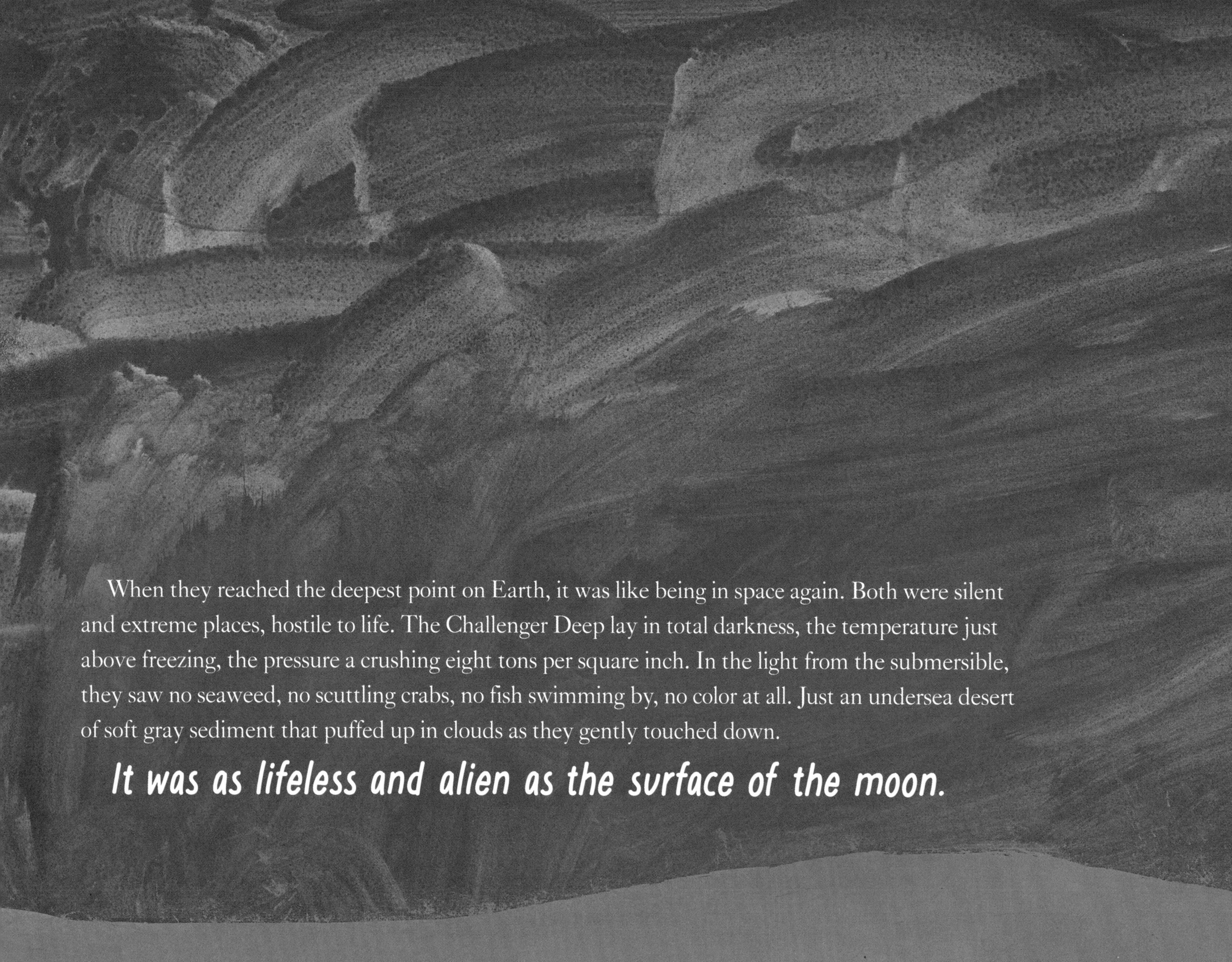

When they reached the deepest point on Earth, it was like being in space again. Both were silent and extreme places, hostile to life. The Challenger Deep lay in total darkness, the temperature just above freezing, the pressure a crushing eight tons per square inch. In the light from the submersible, they saw no seaweed, no scuttling crabs, no fish swimming by, no color at all. Just an undersea desert of soft gray sediment that puffed up in clouds as they gently touched down.

It was as lifeless and alien as the surface of the moon.

TRITON

Kathy remembered the map of the world she'd loved as a child, and how she'd thought it showed everything there was. But, in fact, it was missing *two* other worlds: the one high above Earth and the one where she was now, at the deepest part of the ocean.

And she had seen them all.

Now, as she sat there in the silent darkness at the bottom of the world, she felt a sudden, deep surge of love for the astonishing planet she had studied all her life.

The beautiful planet she called home.

Photo by Space Frontiers/Getty Images

Kathy Sullivan's World Records

The first American woman to walk in space

The first woman to reach the Challenger Deep

The greatest vertical extent traveled by an individual (within Earth's exosphere)

The first person to visit both space and the deepest point on Earth

Glossary

air lock: A sealed compartment with two doors, used to transfer astronauts and cargo between a pressurized spacecraft and the vacuum of outer space

astronaut: Someone who is trained to travel in a spacecraft

extravehicular activity (EVA): Any activity done by an astronaut outside of a spacecraft while in outer space, also known as a spacewalk

galaxy: A vast collection of billions or trillions of stars, planets, gas, dust, and dark matter, held together by gravity

lunar module: A small spacecraft used for transporting astronauts from the main spacecraft to the surface of the moon and back

marine biology: The study of life in oceans, seas, and other saltwater environments

meteoroid: A small rocky or metallic body in outer space

mission: A specific space voyage with defined goals and tasks

National Aeronautics and Space Administration (NASA): A US government agency responsible for the country's space program

National Oceanic and Atmospheric Administration (NOAA): A US government agency responsible for monitoring and predicting changes in Earth's environment

neutral buoyancy pool: A large water-filled pool used to simulate weightlessness when training astronauts for space activities

oceanographer: A scientist who specializes in the study of oceans

orbit: The curved path an object follows around another object due to gravity; usually a smaller object orbits a larger one

planet: A large round celestial body that orbits a star; in our solar system, the planets orbit the sun

satellite: An object that orbits a larger celestial body; usually refers to artificial satellites that were created and launched by humans

Soviet Union (also known as the USSR): A vast country, ruled by the Communist Party, and a powerful rival of the United States that existed from 1922 to 1991; it stretched across Europe and Asia, consisting of fifteen republics, the most important being Russia; in 1991 it was broken up into individual states

submersible: A vehicle that can go underwater

universe: The vast space that contains all of existence, including galaxies, stars, planets, moons, asteroids, and comets

zero gravity: A condition in space where objects and individuals appear to be weightless, because gravity is weaker in space than on Earth

Time Line

October 3, 1951: Kathryn Dwyer Sullivan is born in Paterson, New Jersey.

October 4, 1957: The Soviet satellite Sputnik 1 is launched into low Earth orbit, beginning a Space Race between the United States and the Soviet Union.

1958: Kathy and her family move to the San Fernando Valley in California.

October 1, 1958: The National Aeronautics and Space Administration (NASA) is created by President Dwight D. Eisenhower to compete with the successful Soviet space program.

April 9, 1959: The first group of American astronauts, known as the Mercury Seven, are announced.

April 12, 1961: Soviet cosmonaut Yuri Gagarin becomes the first human to travel into space.

May 5, 1961: Alan B. Shepard Jr. becomes the first American to travel into space, on the Mercury spacecraft *Freedom 7*.

June 16, 1963: Soviet cosmonaut Valentina Tereshkova becomes the first woman to travel into space.

July 20, 1969: The historic Apollo 11 mission successfully lands two American astronauts, Neil Armstrong and Buzz Aldrin, on the surface of the moon.

1973: Kathy graduates from the University of California, Santa Cruz, with a bachelor of science degree in earth sciences.

January 1978: Kathy is chosen for NASA's first class of astronauts to include women.

May 1978: Kathy receives her PhD in geology from Dalhousie University in Nova Scotia, Canada.

June 1978: Kathy arrives at NASA's Lyndon B. Johnson Space Center to begin her astronaut training.

October 5–13, 1984: Kathy flies her first mission. On October 11, she and her crewmate Dave Leestma perform a three-and-a-half-hour extravehicular activity (EVA) as part of their eight-day mission on the space shuttle *Challenger*, making Kathy the first American woman to walk in space.

April 24–29, 1990: Kathy serves on a five-day mission on the space shuttle *Discovery*, successfully deploying the Hubble Space Telescope and setting a shuttle altitude record of 380 miles above Earth.

March 24–April 2, 1992: Kathy flies her third and final mission, on the space shuttle *Atlantis*, having spent a total of more than 532 hours in space.

March 6, 2014: Kathy becomes the undersecretary of commerce for oceans and atmosphere as well as the administrator of the National Oceanic and Atmospheric Administration (NOAA).

November 2019: Kathy's book, *Handprints on Hubble: An Astronaut's Story of Invention*, is published by the MIT Press.

June 7, 2020: Kathy becomes the first woman to dive to the Challenger Deep in the Mariana Trench, the deepest known part of the ocean.

Sources

Burgess, Colin. *Oceans to Orbit: The Story of Australia's First Man in Space, Dr. Paul Scully-Power*. Sydney: Playright Publishing, 1995.

Collins, Eileen M., and Jonathan H. Ward. *Through the Glass Ceiling to the Stars: The Story of the First American Woman to Command a Space Mission*. New York: Arcade Publishing, 2021.

Cooper, Kelly-Leigh. "Kathy Sullivan: The Woman Who's Made History in Sea and Space." BBC News, June 13, 2020.

McGreevy, Nora. "Astronaut Kathy Sullivan Becomes First Woman to Reach Deepest Part of the Ocean." *Smithsonian Magazine*, June 10, 2020.

NASA. "Biographical Data: Kathryn D. Sullivan." April 2014.

Neal, Valerie. "America's First Spacewalking Woman: Kathryn D. Sullivan." National Air and Space Museum, October 11, 2014.

Sullivan, Kathryn D. *Handprints on Hubble: An Astronaut's Story of Invention*. The MIT Press: Cambridge, Massachusetts, 2019.

Sullivan, Kathryn D. "NASA Johnson Space Center Oral History Project: Edited Oral History Transcript, Kathryn D. Sullivan." Interview by Jennifer Ross-Nazzal. May 10, 2007.

Sullivan, Kathryn. "Q&A with Kathryn Sullivan." Interview by Susan Swain. C-SPAN, January 28, 2020.

Sullivan, Kathy. "Kathy Sullivan: Spacewalker." Interview by Chuck Rosenberg. *The Oath*, podcast, June 24, 2020.

Resources for Young Readers

NASA. "STS-45 Mission Highlights." August 28, 2023. Video, 15:42. https://plus.nasa.gov/video/sts-45-mission-highlights.

Scott, Elaine. *Adventure in Space: The Flight to Fix the Hubble*. New York: Hyperion Books for Children, 1995.

Scott, Elaine. *Close Encounters: Exploring the Universe with the Hubble Space Telescope*. New York: Hyperion Books for Children, 1998.

Scott, Elaine. *Space, Stars, and the Beginning of Time: What the Hubble Telescope Saw*. New York: Clarion Books, 2011.

Van Vleet, Carmella, and Dr. Kathy Sullivan. *To the Stars! The First American Woman to Walk in Space*. Illustrated by Nicole Wong. Watertown, MA: Charlesbridge, 2016.